Patrick Kearney:

The True Story of The Freeway Killer

by Jack Rosewood

**Historical Serial Killers and Murderers
True Crime by Evil Killers
Volume 18**

Copyright © 2016 by Wiq Media

ALL RIGHTS RESERVED

No part of this book may be reproduced, stored in a retrieval system, or transmitted in any form or by any means, electronic, mechanical, photocopying, recording, scanning, or otherwise, without the prior written permission of the publisher.

ISBN-13: 978-1535044639

DISCLAIMER:

This serial killer biography includes quotes from those closely involved in the case of American serial killer Patrick Wayne Kearney, also known as the Trash Bag Killer, and it is not the author's intention to defame or intentionally hurt anyone involved. The interpretation of the events leading up to Kearney's arrest and capture are the author's as a result of researching the true crime murder. Any comments made about the psychopathic or sociopathic behavior of Kearney – one of the most prolific murderers in California history - are the sole opinion and responsibility of the person quoted.

Free Bonus!

Get two free books when you sign up to my VIP newsletter at

www.jackrosewood.com

150 interesting trivia about serial killers and the story of serial killer Herbert Mullin.

Contents

Introduction 1

CHAPTER 1: Murder in the making 4

CHAPTER 2: Murder and a descent into madness 10

CHAPTER 3: Parents face worst nightmares 15

CHAPTER 4: A sick obsession 23

CHAPTER 5: A bad time to be gay 28

CHAPTER 6: When Kearney went hunting 36

CHAPTER 7: A confession brings horror to an end 44

CHAPTER 8: Why necrophilia? 56

CHAPTER 9: Parole becomes a nightmare for police and families 61

CHAPTER 10: Confession recanted 64

CHAPTER 11: A survivor tells his story 69

Notable: 76

Conclusion 77

More books by Jack Rosewood 81

GET THESE BOOKS FOR FREE 87

The making of a serial killer 91

A Note From The Author 116

Introduction

Patrick Wayne Kearney was eight years old when he began having fantasies of murder.

And you know how it can be with fantasies. Sometimes, the imagination satisfies, and other times, it only accentuates the hunger.

Kearney was hungry, and that need of his was eventually going to be sated.

The oldest of three boys, Kearney was born on September 24, 1939, in Los Angeles, to parents George and Eunice Kearney. George was a member of the Los Angeles Police Department, while Eunice stayed home to care for the children, Patrick and his younger brothers, Michael and Chester.

The City of Angels was a lucky place for a kid to grow up, or would have been, had the future serial killer not been sickly as a child, which made him an easy target for school bullies.

Despite having an IQ of 180 – which makes him, psychologists say, a genius – he was unable to find ways to win over his peers, even after his parents moved to Arizona, where he switched schools and had access to a new group of classmates.

But everything's hotter in Arizona, and so was the bullying Kearney faced at his new school. The bullies were the same, and Kearney was still an easy target.

Later on, after college and a stint in the military, Kearney gave marriage a try, but the short-lived union ended in divorce.

Then, as fortune would have it, he met the man who would eventually become his longtime lover, and when Kearney fled back to California to start over yet again, his new partner David Hill soon followed.

As an adult, Kearney had developed into a man with the buttoned-up look of an accountant, sort of like New Jersey's John List, who was a fugitive for almost 18 years after murdering his entire family and moving across the country to take on a new identity. Kearney appeared mild-mannered and studious, and the electrical engineer could have had it made. He landed an engineering job at Hughes Aircraft, founded by none other than the eccentric and successful Howard Hughes, whose friends and lovers included Katharine Hepburn, Bette Davis, Ava Gardner, Olivia de Havilland, Ginger Rogers, Gene Tierney and Joan Fontaine.

But Kearney couldn't really shake that troubled childhood of his, no matter what good fortune later came his way.

While he didn't learn to hobnob with the rich and famous during his years at Hughes Aircraft, he did take away one thing from his time in California. He learned that his buttoned-up looks were appealing enough to some of the young men who were part of the burgeoning gay scene, and Kearney took advantage of it.

Unfortunately for many of those boys and young men, usually thin and blond with side-swept long hair, they resembled Kearney's childhood bullies and they would be the ones forced to pay for the others' torment, as Kearney's fantasies festered and finally burst open in a bloody torrent of gunshots, necrophilia and dismemberment.

"This guy's got a master's degree in murder," said Los Angeles County detective Louis Danoff.

CHAPTER 1:
Murder in the making

Growing up, Patrick Wayne Kearney described his childhood as comparable to the nightmare youth suffered by fictional teen Carrie White in the Stephen King novel of a high school prom gone wrong. The story was brought to life on the silver screen in a movie starring Sissy Spacek, who sought deadly revenge on her fellow students after being drenched in pig's blood while wearing the homecoming queen crown.

The oldest of three boys, Kearney did not get the luck of the draw, and was a slight, effeminate, wimpy little boy who wore glasses with thick lenses. His classmates didn't let him forget any of it for a minute. His fellow students called him "girly-boy," "queer boy" and "little faggot."

Unfortunately, the cruel bullying was occurring during some of the most important, formative years of Kearney's life.

The consequences of bullying

Bullying has long been linked to criminal behavior, in part because the emotions and experiences that shape our thinking are for the most part formulated in our younger say.

Not only do our experiences as youth shape how we t they also shape how we see ourselves, since peers have the most influence on our self-esteem.

In 1902, sociologist Charles H. Cooley suggested that our perception of ourselves comes from how others see us, and our peers' opinions essentially represent a "mirror image" of ourselves.

As for Kearney's looking glass?

"As a kid he was often beat up by others since he was small and called queer by his peers though he was interested in girls," said psychiatrist John McMullen.

Kearney eventually established a long-term romance with a man, so it could be his classmates saw something in him that he himself did not, or that their cruel words sparked ideas at a time when he was developing sexually.

Somebody would pay

While it's likely that during the time he was being bullied, he outwardly did what most tortured children do - which is to not only pretend not to hear the words, but to also pretend they don't hurt - inside, Kearney seethed, and he had no intention of forgetting any of the pain his classmates caused him.

as being teased and tormented by ng his fantasies of murder, which ed and heinous with every passing

e at greater risk for later criminal activity, ... ra Finley, an Assistant Professor of Sociology and Criminology at Barry University. "Studies have shown victims may act out later in life as a way to feel powerful. Many victims become the aggressor."

For Kearney, whose torment seemed relentless, aggression was putting it mildly.

Kearney's simmering rage took hold early, and by early adulthood it had boiled over.

He was desperate for revenge, and there was likely no turning back once his fantasies of murder became linked with sex – the ultimate power play for someone who has felt like an underdog for much of his life.

His later actions would suggest that for Kearney, those endless unpleasant experiences with his peers developed into a self-loathing that eventually turned outward. Unable to exact revenge on his tormenters, he instead found targets that served as stand-ins or substitutes for those who had bullied him.

If he couldn't go back in time to make his bullies pay, he would find someone else to make things right. Targeting young gay men also allowed him to kill some part of himself that caused him immense hatred.

A dangerous outlet

Of course, his rage might have come out in some different, less deadly, way had his father not purchased a .22 caliber rifle to hunt animals when Kearney was just 13. Even at this early age, burgeoning on adolescence, it wasn't animals Kearney was planning on hunting.

His father also gave him some hunting tips, and told him that the ideal place to shoot a pig was above and behind the left ear, which would result in the least amount of blood and would better ensure a kill as the bullet was likely to lodge in the brain.

Kearney used these tips to perfect his skills on animals, all the while fantasizing about killing humans, instead. He must have found the idea arousing, because he also later confessed that he had had his first sexual experience around the same time, albeit with the family dog.

Kearney switched schools when he entered junior high, but a new school – this time the Diane S. Leichman Special Education Center – didn't mean less abuse. Physically he hadn't changed, and it's possible his classmates could tell somehow that he was the type to fuck the family pet.

As any bullied student will know, school days were hell for Patrick Wayne Kearney.

It was just as well, then, that George decided to leave the LAPD and become a salesman with a travel agency, a job that would mean moving the family to Arizona.

This time, although still faced with bullying at school, Kearney was better able to ignore the abuse, and he immersed himself in his education, where he developed a love of languages and became fairly fluent in Spanish, Japanese and Chinese.

After graduating from high school, Kearney attended El Camino Community College in Torrance, California, where he studied engineering.

After graduation in 1958, he joined the U.S. Air Force, hoping to travel the world and put his education to good use overseas, but instead of some exotic locale like he'd hoped, he instead found himself stationed in Texas.

Life, luck, changes

There was some luck to be had, however, because in 1960, just before receiving an honorable discharge from the Air Force, he met David Hill, a high school dropout from Lubbock, Texas, who had been discharged from the army for an undisclosed personality disorder, presumed to be homosexuality, which was considered by the military to be a mental disorder and disallowed within its ranks.

The two were immediately attracted to one another, despite Hill's high school sweetheart turned wife back at home.

Hill was tall and muscular with the looks of a construction worker. He was the antithesis of Kearney, who at 5'5" was much shorter and skinny, like the teen getting sand kicked in his face in those old Charles Atlas ads in the backs of comic books.

But in this case – like in many relationships – opposites attracted, and the two began what would be a tumultuous on-again, off-again love affair that lasted 15 years, even as Hill struggled to choose between his wife and his gay lover.

Eventually Kearney tired of Texas and decided to return to California, maybe to escape the sweltering Texas heat, and in 1961, Hill chose to follow. The two settled in Long Beach, and Kearney's life was finally looking up.

It wouldn't be long, however, before Hill began feeling restless, and after about a year, Hill left Kearney to hitchhike around the country, eventually making his way back to his wife in Lubbock.

CHAPTER 2:
Murder and a descent into madness

Looking for anything to push pass the pain of his loss, 22-year-old Kearney began taking history classes at California State University at Long Beach, but soon found that nothing really distracted him.

For Kearney, the rejection was monumental, and it unleashed a hotbed of pent-up rage that resulted in a campaign of death that would last for more than a decade.

Losing his lover brought back all of Kearney's childhood aggressions, and he began taking them out on hapless young men he encountered along the way.

The first victim, a 19-year-old from either Louisiana or Oklahoma, made the mistake of accepting a ride on Kearney's motorcycle. As soon as they were somewhere secluded, Kearney put his hunting lessons to use and shot the young man in the back of the head, behind the left ear like his police officer father had taught him.

Kearney then had some fun, sodomizing and mutilating the young man's body before abandoning it out somewhere off of California State Route 86.

The second murder was an act of protection on Kearney's part, because his first victim's 16-year-old cousin had seen the older teen ride off with him, and the older man didn't want to leave behind any witnesses.

In order to protect himself, Kearney returned to the place he'd picked up his first victim and enticed the younger cousin to also go for a ride. It would be the last decision the teen would make.

An 18-year-old named Mike would be the next to die, but David Hill's return would quiet Kearney's rage and bring this first string of murders to an end.

It was 1963, and Kearney landed that dream job at Hughes Aircraft, founded in 1932 by Howard Hughes. His new position not only came with prestigious, but also a generous paycheck. To celebrate, the lovers moved to Culver City, where they found a place not far from the movie studio that had once housed Desilu Productions.

Coworkers later said Kearney was an exemplary employee. A "model worker," said one.

Murders become more dangerous and detailed

In 1966, David Hill and his wife Linda finally divorced, and for almost two years, things were completely normal in the Kearney-Hill household.

This is, until the spring of 1967, when the two went to Tijuana, Mexico, where they ran into one of Hill's old friends, George, who invited them to stay at his place for the duration of their vacation. It would be a fatal mistake for George, because Kearney was a rather nasty houseguest.

Instead of being appreciative of having a place to stay, Kearney shot George as the man slept in his master bedroom, then dragged the body into the bathtub, first for sex, then to dismember him. He also painstakingly skinned the body with an X-Acto knife and removed the bullet from George's head to lessen his chances of being caught. He then buried the remains both in George's backyard as well as behind the garage.

It has been taking a chance to kill George while Hill was in the house, especially given the time Kearney had spent with the body. But perhaps the thrill of discovery was also something that excited him, or maybe Hill knew about the murders all the while, despite Kearney's later admission that Hill had had nothing to do with any of his crimes.

We may never know if Hill knew what was going on in the night while they were visiting his friend George.

And as for the man from Tijuana, his remains would not be discovered for a decade.

California dreams turn to dust

Something about the murder of George – nerves, the fear of getting caught or possibly, Hill's anger if he had in fact been a witness to any part of the grisly murder scene – made Kearney decide to lie low for a bit, and he bought a house in Redondo Beach, spending just over $20,000 on the purchase.

While he anticipated a love nest, he and Hill fought often, and whenever they did, Kearney jumped into his Volkswagen Beetle and headed back to Tijuana, where he is believed to have killed several more men, dismembering them and disposing of their bodies in trash bags.

Kearney eventually went off the rails when he awoke one morning to find Hill gone again, this time only leaving behind a note.

His only way to vent his rage was to kill, but it would be almost 10 years before any evidence from Kearney's revenge killings would be noticed.

And by then, the overwhelming number of bodies turning up along California's highways – Randy Kraft and William Bonin were also trolling the state for young men they often dumped along the roadside like so much trash – had become a nightmare for California's police force.

Blood is the drug

By 1974, Kearney was addicted to the thrill of killing, and his murder rate had escalated to at least one victim a month.

As his rate increased, his patterns evolved.

He either picked up unsuspected hitchhikers or trolled gay bars and bathhouses in search of men who were bigger than he was, allowing him the thrill of being in control after all those years as a child when he wasn't.

He usually didn't waste any time, and once they were in his vehicle, Kearney shot them with a Derringer .22 pistol, leaving them slumped over in the passenger seat as if they were sleeping as he drove somewhere secluded where he could rape their dead bodies.

He later told police he shot his victims while they were asleep or distracted, and chose to shoot them behind the ear "because they did not bleed much when shot there."

Kearney rarely left the corpses where he sodomized them. Instead he would bring them home to drain their blood and dismember the bodies, placing the remains in industrial-strength plastic trash bags that he would either dump in the desert, along California's less traveled freeways, in the canyons behind Los Angeles or beneath tons of trash in area landfills.

CHAPTER 3:
Parents face worst nightmares

On August 24, 1974, five-year-old Ronald Dean Smith was late for dinner.

He'd been playing in the park with a friend, and although the other boy was at home, Ronnie had failed to make it back to his grandmother's house, where he was staying while his mom was out of town.

As it got later, Shirley O'Conner began to panic, and she called the Los Angeles County Sheriff's Lennox Substation to report her missing grandson.

Police learned that the two boys had been playing in the park's sandbox when they got into what the little boy called "a sand fight." He had gone home to clean up, while Ronnie, in tears, remained at the park.

Police immediately searched the park and interviewed neighbors in a door-to-door canvass, but nothing turned up. It was as if Ronnie Smith had vanished into thin air.

"There were no clues. Nothing," said Lt. Ray Gott. "The boy had just disappeared."

A week after Ronnie's disappearance, his divorced mother, 22-year-old Joann O'Connor, made a heartfelt plea for the return of her son at an emotional press conference she held at the police station.

"The reason we wanted you all to come here is to tell whoever had Ronnie how much we want him back. We definitely do feel in our hearts that he's alive and OK and that he's safe. I just want to tell whoever he's with now that he's very important to me, that he's... he's all I've got. And that I love him so very much. I know that whoever took Ronnie took him because they wanted a little boy to love, and I know you took him because he's so beautiful and that you won't hurt him."

If only she'd been right about her assumptions.

On Sunday, October 13, 1974, almost two months after Ronnie's disappearance, some kids were collecting cans along Riverside County's Ortega Highway when they discovered the body of a badly decomposed young boy.

The Riverside County Sheriff's Department was soon on the scene, and based upon the clothing the corpse was wearing, along with an autopsy, they realized they'd found the missing 5-year-old Smith boy.

There were no suspects in the boy's death, although police later learned that the boy had been held for two days and was raped and tortured before being killed, suggesting that Kearney's rage was especially out of control during that time.

Another family faces horror

Stephen Demchik always held out hope that his 13-year-old son John, had gone to San Francisco – the birthplace of bands such as the Grateful Dead, Jefferson Airplane, Big Brother and the Holding Company, and one of the most gay-friendly cities in the United States - when he disappeared on June 26, 1975.

He had been standing on a corner in Inglewood when Kearney offered to give him a ride home.

But instead of taking the teen home, Kearney shot Demchik in the head as soon as the boy got into his truck, then drove 15 miles southeast of Calexico along the California-Mexico border, a secluded area where he was able to drag his unconscious victim from the truck, undress him, rape him and leave him to die. No one knows how long Demchik was lying in the dirt, bloody, naked and in pain.

Not knowing any of this, Stephen Demchik told his wife, Norma, and John's four siblings that he had found a better job in San Francisco, and would be moving there for a while. In reality, he was desperately searching for his son.

"I figured he might be up in San Francisco," Demchik said. "I used to spend my weekends just driving around the city and on the highways just to see if I could spot him."

The disappearance of his son haunted his desperate father.

"I dreamed of him up there," Demchik said. "The last dream I had, he was in a dungeon. He was calling me, 'Come and get me.' I asked him, `Where are you?' He never answered me. I went through a lot of hell."

It would be six years before Demchik's abused body was discovered, and that would only be because Kearney had confessed to the murder and told police where he's left the boy to die.

Demchik was identified by his mother, who was shown a scrap of clothing he'd been wearing on the day that he disappeared.

In was devastating for the mother, and after that, John's sister said, "I think she just didn't want to go on."

Norma died not long after identifying her son's clothing.

Decades later, Stephen Demchik was living in the same house, but with his wife and son dead, his four other children grown, it was nothing like a real home, especially given that it had once been one that had been filled with so much love and laughter.

A photo in a frame and too few memories are all Demchik had left.

"He's not coming back. There's nothing that can bring him back. I knew that after the police called and his mother identified his clothes. I said, 'That's him. There's no use grieving over it anymore.'"

But still, he can't help himself from reliving his pain, especially on John's important days.

"There are times when I remember him on his birthday or at Christmas. That's hard.

But I have to reach back and say, 'He's not coming back.'"

No matter how hard he tries, Stephen continues to grieve what Kearney callously stole from him.

Troubled boy meets sad fate

"I thought my world was coming to an end when my son was murdered," said Elizabeth McGhee, whose 13-year-old son Michael was one of Kearney's victims.

While Michael had a cherub's face, the boy with the brown hair and sweet smile was often in trouble. His short life was punctuated by truancy and a host of crimes.

The local cops were well aware of the boy, who'd dropped out of school at age 12 in favor of burglary, car theft and other offenses, including incorrigibility (incapable of being corrected or amended, essentially a juvenile delinquent).

His sister called him a "rebellious teenager."

Michael had met Kearney in early June of 1976 when he had picked him up hitchhiking and invited him to go camping with him at his favorite spots, Lake Elsinore.

McGhee almost slipped out of Kearney's clutches, since he was unable to go that time, but the boy made the mistake of telling Kearney to ask him again later. Because of that fateful car ride and conversation, McGhee wouldn't make it past his 13th birthday.

The next week, McGhee's sister opened the door when Kearney stopped by, and although she told the older man, "a little guy" in glasses wearing camouflage, that her brother was grounded and couldn't go camping with him, McGhee was slipping out the back door even as his sister and Kearney were talking.

Kearney left, but McGhee ran to catch up.

Michael McGhee's brother, Robert, tried to stop the 13-year-old from going off with Kearney, but that day – June 16, 1976 – was the last day any of the McGhees saw young, incorrigible Michael.

Another family faces heartache

Decades after his death, a page devoted to 8-year-old Merle Chance, who went by the name of Hondo, was peppered with notes of love from his classmates, who never forgot the dark-haired boy with the sweet smile.

"You will always be my friend," said one post, while another showcased the boy's sense of right and wrong, justice and evil.

"Hondo was a brave and helpful child who protected my brother from awful bullies that were much older. If he had not been murdered and had been allowed to live I can only imagine the strength of character and wonderful things he could have done. He had a heart of gold," another friend added.

One girl, a year younger than Hondo, remembered the boy as her protector, four decades after his ill-fated encounter with Patrick Wayne Kearney.

"My best friend as a small child, he was my hero, with his large heart and protective spirit. I loved to see him ride his bike up and he always looked after me, because no one else did. I have searched for years for a picture or some celebration of him (I was seven years old when he was taken), and to see the celebration of him is such a blessing. He will forever be 'looking out' for all of those he loved left that are still behind. He will always be in my heart, for his spirit is what saved me in many ways...Thank you Hondo. You made such a difference in my life."

Hondo's death decimated his family. His mother, Bertha, carries the blame for the death of her son, who vanished on April 6, 1977, when he was riding his bike in Kearney's neighborhood.

Kearney took him home and smothered him, then sodomized the small corpse, which he later dumped in Angeles National Forest, where Hondo became a true angel.

"I had four other kids, but he was my baby," said Chance. "I can't describe what it made me feel like. For a long time, it wasn't easy. It was not easy. I stayed by myself every day. I went out to his grave every day. I would take flowers and sit and talk to him. If people saw me, they thought I was crazy because I was sitting there talking to a headstone."

Her husband blamed her, too, she added.

"He got real cold to me the day they said they found our son. He blamed me for his disappearance and his death. He said if I hadn't bought him his bicycle it wouldn't have happened. I guess he had to blame somebody."

CHAPTER 4:
A sick obsession

Patrick Kearney was hiding a lot of sick secrets, especially so his interest in Houston Heights serial killer Dean Corll, a Texas madman who bribed two boys in his neighborhood with booze and weed to bring their friends over to his place "to party." The only one having any fun, however, was the sadistic Corll, who had a torture board that kept his victims from escaping while he tortured them – sometimes amputating their penises while they writhed in pain on the blood-soaked slab of wood – sodomized them repeatedly and finally, when his fun was over, killed them.

Most were buried at a boat storage shed Corll rented, and the night detectives dug up the bodies was one that never left them.

Corll had wrapped the bodies in plastic that he'd put down beneath the board to catch any blood or entrails as he tortured his victims, and then covered them in a dusting of lime. The lime, however, had helped speed decomposition, and eventually as detectives dug deeper, they were only finding body parts or bones simmering in a putrid gelatinous liquid.

"It was a hot day, and the smell would just knock you over," said Houston Post photographer Jerry Click.

Sgt. David Mullican of the Pasadena Police Department still remembered the smell, almost 40 years later, as he remembered while giving an interview over lunch with Texas Monthly magazine.

"I can go back to that first day at the storage unit when we started digging," he said, "and just like that, the smell comes back to me, the smell of all those rotting ..."

Mullican was unable to finish his sentence, or his meal that day.

It was sick stuff, and Kearney reveled in it, collecting as many newspaper clippings about Corll's murders as he could find.

Hillside Stranglers

While Dean Corll's terrorizing of Texas was Kearney's favorite bit of news, he also followed the Hillside Stranglers, who were operating in Los Angeles between October of 1977 and February of 1978.

While police always knew they were dealing with two killers, since cousins Kenneth Bianchi and Angelo Buono both left semen at the scene, they didn't immediately let on to the press that there were two men at work in the Hollywood Hills.

It was Buono who was the leader of the two, and in order to encourage his cousin to participate in the crimes, he told him, "You can't let a cunt get the upper hand. Put them in their place."

Because Kearney killed to also put people "in their place," he likely related to the rage that guided these two monsters as they sought out more victims.

While initially the two worked as pimps and forced two runaway girls to prostitute themselves or face severe beatings, eventually they weren't satisfied with simple rape and torture. And once they graduated to murder, they were almost unstoppable, killing three young prostitutes in a matter of three weeks, then kidnapping two young girls off a school bus to rape and strangle a week later.

In the end, the two were convicted of raping, torturing and murdering 10 females between the ages of 12 and 28.

From them, Kearney likely decided age didn't matter, which would explain the varied ages of his victims.

They received life sentences.

The Zodiac Killer

Police have been looking for the Zodiac Killer since 1969, and Patrick Kearney has been following their progress.

Between December of 1968 and October of 1969, a mere eight-month period, at least four men and three women were killed by a monster who sent a series of letters containing cryptograms to the Vallejo Times Herald, the San Francisco Chronicle and The San Francisco Examiner, demanding front page attention or he would kill again.

While the Zodiac Killer – a name the mystery murderer gave himself – lay claim to 37 murders, only seven were directly linked.

Of the four cryptograms sent to the newspapers, only one has been decoded.

It contained misspellings along with a few letters that were never deciphered, but it helped explain what the Zodiac Killer was all about.

"I LIKE KILLING PEOPLE BECAUSE IT IS SO MUCH FUN IT IS MORE FUN THAN KILLING WILD GAME IN THE FORREST BECAUSE MAN IS THE MOST DANGEROUE ANAMAL OF ALL TO KILL SOMETHING GIVES ME THE MOST THRILLING EXPERENCE IT IS EVEN BETTER THAN GETTING YOUR ROCKS OFF WITH A GIRL THE BEST PART OF IT IS THAE WHEN I DIE I WILL BE REBORN IN PARADICE AND THEI HAVE KILLED WILL BECOME MY SLAVES I WILL NOT GIVE YOU MY NAME BECAUSE YOU WILL TRY TO SLOI DOWN OR ATOP MY COLLECTIOG OF SLAVES FOR MY AFTERLIFE EBEORIETEMETHHPITI," it read.

All of the letters from the attention-seeking Zodiac were signed with a circle with an X superimposed on top. Some included bits of evidence from crime scenes to prove the connection.

It was demented, and that alone made it an obsession for the dark, twisted little man who turned childhood torment, something many kids endure without breaking down into madness, into a reason to kill.

CHAPTER 5:
A bad time to be gay

In the late 1970s, just when Kearney was perfecting his murderous modus operandi, former beauty queen and orange juice spokeswoman Anita Bryant had just made headlines across the nation for succeeding in shutting down gay rights efforts across the nation, using the argument that many gay men prey on young boys, making them a risk to society in the roles of teachers or Boy Scout leaders.

"What these people really want, hidden behind obscure legal phrases, is the legal right to propose to our children that theirs is an acceptable alternate way of life. [...] I will lead such a crusade to stop it as this country has not seen before," she said in 1977 as part of her discriminatory "Save Our Children" campaign, which was backed by religious leaders including Jerry Falwell, who regularly ended up being featured as "Asshole of the Month" in Larry Flynt's graphic political/porn publication Hustler.

"As a mother, I know that homosexuals cannot biologically reproduce children; therefore, they must recruit our children," she said, and with those words was ultimately able to bring about the repeal of a Florida law banning discrimination against the gay community.

"If gays are granted rights, next we'll have to give rights to prostitutes and to people who sleep with St. Bernards and to nail biters," she added.

While Bryant's hate campaign prevailed in Florida, the gay community retaliated by boycotting orange juice and raising money for their own campaign.

Meanwhile, Patrick Kearney was taking advantage of the gay men living across the country in California, where many men had fled looking for a more accepting place to live.

Among Kearney's favorite hunting grounds were gay cruising areas including Hollywood's Selma Avenue and MacArthur Park in Los Angeles, and as his victims began turning up, along with those of the other two men preying on the region's gay men, the press had a field day.

Are gay men more apt to kill?

While the 1970s were a time of both freedom and oppression for the gay community, a growing body of experts was quick to protest the idea that gay men were more likely to be predators than their straight counterparts, despite the escalating body count turning up along California's highways.

"When it's a homosexual who kills ten people or twelve, or whatever, the headline is HOMOSEXUAL KILLS. It sticks in your mind. You never get the headline HETEROSEXUAL KILLS," said Robert Gould, a professor of psychiatry at New York Medical College who estimates that heterosexuals and homosexuals are likely to murder at a similar rate.

Others suggested that gays were more likely to kill than heterosexuals, but there were experts to dispute those claims.

"I don't think there is anything inherent in homosexuality that makes them disturbed people," Judd Marmor, past president of the American Psychiatric Association, told Time magazine.

Still, the turmoil caused by the stigma of being gay, especially when coupled with bullying at school at a young, impressionable age— could cause problems that aren't inherently related to homosexuality itself, but manifest themselves because of it. That's especially true when gays feel a sense of self-hatred because they are unable to accept their own homosexuality.

"I think you will find more disturbed homosexuals. The extra fillip of pathology in the homosexual is due to cultural opposition and discrimination," said Gould.

Homosexuals as targets

At the time when so many gay men were turning up dead alongside California's highways, experts suggested one of the reasons could be related to the amplified aggression that's potentially present between two men in a romantic relationship. But still, they said, the most common reason for attacks on gay men – at least in the 1970s – was the inherent danger of sexual hookups between total strangers, a common part of the gay scene.

"Homosexuals are an easy population to get access to in some anonymous way," said Berkeley psychologist Michael Evans.

"Gays are easy prey," said Chicago Police Sgt. Richard Sandberg.

And California – with its beaches and anonymity and promise – was a big draw, especially given a new 1975 law repealing a statute making homosexuality between consenting adults a crime.

Murders damages civil rights efforts

Still, the climate was such that many people remained closeted, and at a time when gay advocacy groups were struggling to overcome Anita Bryant's message of intolerance, news of the Trash Bag Killings was hardly beneficial.

"The timing obviously couldn't have been worse," Peter G. Fritsch, an organizer of a successful homosexual political action committee, told the magazine The Advocate. "A lot of money has to be raised, and it is hard to raise money when people are fearful. A murder like this one sends people back to their closets in droves."

It also helped further Bryant's discriminatory cause by preying upon people's fears.

"These murders have reminded people that the Houston murders [Dean Corll] were homosexually oriented and that there are many crimes involving homosexuals," said Orange County State Sen. John Briggs, who campaigned with Anita Bryant in Florida. "It has reminded them that there was a sexual strain in the Corona [Juan Corona, who killed 25 migrant workers in 1971] murders."

"The effect on us," says Fritsch, "is something like what would it be if you had a black man arrested for murdering 10 white people during a civil rights drive in the '60s. There's just no way it can help."

Hitchhiking made murder easier

For the young people who were lured to California for its free-spirited, Haight-Ashbury vibe, hitchhiking was usually the transportation mode of choice.

For the estimated five percent of gay men who become predators, mostly because of a deep-seated hatred for themselves and their sexual preferences, having such easy access to so many young people was beyond enticing, and

Kearney was among the serial killers who couldn't resist the draw.

And because hitchhikers are usually far away from anyone who knows them intimately, their killers are long gone and on to a new victim before anyone even notices the first victim went missing.

"During the '70s and early '80s, more than a hundred young hitchhikers caught rides on the streets and freeways of southern California and didn't live to tell about it," said Dennis McDougal, author of the book "Angel of Darkness."

If they did survive their travel as hitchhikers, many soon learned that survival was tricky in the Golden State, and some found themselves turning to prostitution to make enough money to pay for food, drugs, housing or anything else they might need. Of course that made them as vulnerable as they were when they were on the open road, their thumb out bumming a ride.

In 1980, a year after Patrick Kearney was behind bars, police made it painfully clear how high the murder rate was in California, especially given the number of serial killers at work. (The state comes in fourth for total number of serial killers, surpassed only by Florida, Nevada and Alaska, which takes the top spot, likely due to the long, dark winters that have to drive people crazy.)

"In this county alone, we have 30 to 40 dumps every year," said Los Angeles County Sheriff's Captain Walt Ownbey.

A deadly stretch of highway

There's a section of California Route 74 known as Ortega Highway that has been a favorite dumping ground for dead bodies for years.

Between Orange County and Lake Elsinore, where Patrick Kearney loved to go camping, the 44-mile stretch of roadway has been used by many notorious killers, including William Bonin, the infamous "Co-Ed Killer," who dumped at least four of his victims along the desolate stretch of highway. (For a time, Bonin shared the name the Freeway Killer with Patrick Kearney while police sorted out the killer responsible for the growing pile of bodies.)

Even Randy Kraft, the killer who kept the title Freeway Killer after Bonin and Kearney were renamed, visited a restaurant along this stretch of road, ordering an avocado sandwich and a Coke at El Cariso Mountain Restaurant.

But Trash Bag Killer Kearney got there first, and dumped one of his victims there, stuffed into an industrial-sized trash bag, in 1977.

"There are shallow graves out here that just haven't been discovered," California Highway Patrol Officer Steve Miles told the Los Angeles Times in 2009 from the comfort of his patrol car. "People will do anything out here."

It's the stuff of both real and imagined nightmares, added true crime writer Dennis McDougal.

Ortega Highway, he said, "is this kind of unique strip of remote, undeveloped and primitive real estate for people of ill intentions. It gained this dark, negative reputation as a place where evil could be done with impunity."

Sadistic and prolific

When gay serial killers kill because of their inability to accept their sexuality, it comes with exaggerated rage, making them prone to what Harold Schechter, a true crime writer who specializes in serial killers, calls "overkill."

Gay serial killers like Kearney usually take sadistic pleasure in the torture, mutilation or dismemberment of their victims. In Kearney's case, however, he rarely tortured his victims, and only raped, mutilated and dismembered them after they were dead. He saved his torture for his youngest victims.

He did fit the other part of the profile, though. Gay serial killers are also more prolific, Schechter said.

While Kearney was only tried for 21 murders, he confessed to many more, but there was not enough evidence to bring about a conviction.

Based on his confessions, Kearney's total murder count is believed to be as high as 43 victims.

CHAPTER 6:
When Kearney went hunting

For Kearney, the urge to kill most often occurred after he and Hill had had a fight.

He would then take either his Volkswagen Beetle or his truck for long drives, choosing solitary roads for traveling. Along the way, he would pick up his favorite prey – young male hitchhikers, which were pretty prolific during the peace and free love era of the 1970s, or young men he met while cruising the area's gay bars.

It's likely the mild-mannered, nerdy look of Kearney's made him seem quite innocuous and safe, but once in Kearney's car, the young men or boys had little chance, despite Kearney's small stature, because Kearney usually either shot them or strangled them as soon as he was able to catch them off guard.

Kearney was a clean, meticulous, detailed murderer. Once he had killed his victim, most often with a shot to the head, he would drive them to a secluded place as if they were going on a romantic rendezvous, and he would then sodomize their corpses.

Having faced so much rejection during his formative years, its likely Kearney raped his victims after they were dead so they could not reject him. The act also gave him the ultimate sense of power over those victims who resembled his childhood tormenters. By raping them, he put his victims into a submissive role, demonstrating a dominance that he was never able to gain during the years when he was bullied.

After having sex with his victims, Kearney would take them home, wash them, drain the blood from their bodies in the bathtub and dismember them.

He would then neatly wrap the parts in industrial-strength trash bags, getting rid of the remains on his way to work, during lunch or late at night when he was driving around in search of a new victim.

Grisly deeds unearthed

Police began to have an inkling that more than one serial killer was on the loose beginning on April 13, 1975, when the mutilated remains of 21-year-old Albert Rivera turned up near San Juan Capistrano, home to the cliff swallows that return to the region each spring in a flurry of feathered wings and song.

This find stuffed into a trash bag was not completely uncommon in California in 1975, given the sheer number of serial killers who were making the rounds during the 1970s, a time when young people from across the country were moving to California in hopes of a better life, making themselves targets by adopting dangerous lifestyles.

But the neatness of the packaging made Rivera's death different than the others.

"The body was wrapped in a fetal position, using heavy-duty nylon fiber tape," detective Al Sett reported to the district attorney. The body "was then placed in two heavy-duty commercial plastic trash can liners. He was then placed in a common household green plastic trash bag which was also wrapped with tape."

Sett communicated with neighboring police agencies, and found that Orange County had a body found in a trash bag, as did Riverside.

By summer's arrival, eight more bodies had been found, shot and dismembered, each similarly wrapped and strewn like trash through Los Angeles, Imperial, Riverside, San Diego and Orange counties.

Given the similarities, police were able to pin the murders on a singular suspect thanks to the M.O. that was so much like a signature.

All of the victims were gay, all had been found nude, all had been shot in the head with a gun that was a similar make and model, many were dismembered and mutilated and all were stuffed into identical plastic trash bags.

The pattern gave police a certain number of clues, and while they publicly dubbed the perpetrator "The Trash Bag Killer," behind closed doors the case was called "fags in bags," and no one was trying too hard to find the killer.

Then, for almost two years, things were quiet. The down time, however, was too good to be true.

Nightmares in bags

On January 24, 1977, a state employee was working beneath the San Diego Freeway's Lennox tunnel, when he tripped over a tightly-wrapped garbage bag containing something significantly weighty.

It turned out to be 28-year-old Nicolas Hernandez-Jimenez, a Los Angeles prostitute.

Apparently, the Trash Bag Killer had not gone silent after all.

And police were about to close in on him, like it or not.

In death, LaMay helps track a killer

John LaMay, who wore his sandy blond hair long and swept to the side to accommodate a cowlick, was 17 when he left his home in El Segundo for the last time, on March 13, 1977.

"He'd spent the night at a friend's house before without telling me," said LaMay's mother, Patricia LaMay.

Still, he'd never done that on a school night, so she knew instinctively that something was wrong.

Patricia called one of John's friends, a neighbor who said that he'd seen LaMay at about 5:30 p.m. that Sunday evening, and learned that the teen was headed to Redondo Beach to meet a man named Dave, who he'd met at a local gym.

When LaMay arrived at Dave's house sometime after 6 p.m., Hill was not at home, but Kearney invited the teenager to come in and wait for him.

The two watched television for a while, until Kearney pulled out his .22 Derringer and shot LaMay in the back of the head.

He stashed the body in a closet to hide it from Hill, then later, dismembered it, washed and wrapped it, then dumped it in the desert south of Corona.

Five days later, police found John's body, his corpse dismembered and his torso stuffed inside multiple trash bags.

His killer had taken the time to carefully cut his victim up, draining the body of blood and washing the parts before packaging them neatly into five industrial trash bags sealed with ivory nylon tape. Three of the bags were stuffed into a nearby oil drum, while two that apparently didn't fit were discarded on the ground. LaMay's head was missing.

The MO matched the "fag in a bag" killings, but detectives didn't know that in death, John LaMay would give them the clues they needed to stop the ice-cold killer in his tracks.

Searching for a killer

Assigned the case, detectives Al Sett and Roger Wilson began by questioning John's friends, who said the young man liked to hang out with two guys named Pat and Dave, who lived in Redondo Beach.

Further questions led them to the home of Patrick Kearney and Dave Hill. They had an idea what they were looking for, based on evidence they had found on not only John's body, but also on the tape wrapped around the bags he was housed in, including blue fibers.

Kearney and Hill were completely cooperative when police arrived, and expressed shock over the death of their friend John LaMay. They allowed the officers to enter their home, but as they watched them gather evidence, they became more concerned.

Police initially took a sample of carpet fibers from the house, and when it matched fibers found on the tape that sealed the trash bags, they returned again.

This time they painstakingly took samples of Kearney's pubic hair, Hill's pubic hair and the hair of their little white poodle. The men complied, but their concern mounted.

In order to go any further, police needed a warrant, so they returned to the station without Kearney and Hill. When they notified the pair that they now had the warrant they needed and planned a thorough search of their duplex, Kearney tossed all of his revered Dean Corll newspaper clippings, resigned from his job at Hughes Aircraft and the two men fled to Hill's family home back in El Paso, Texas.

When Sett and Wilson arrived with their warrant, they had no idea what kind of hell that had just walked into.

Inside, they found one of their most important bits of evidence - a bloody hacksaw, the one Kearney used to dismember some of his victims, coated in dried bits of John LaMay's flesh and blood.

Using Luminal, they found residual blood all over the bathroom, and in another part of the house, found a roll of nylon filament tape like the tape used on the trash bags to wrap up John LaMay.

A search of Kearney's office at Hughes Aircraft yielded the source of the industrial trash bags linked to at least 20 murders.

Meanwhile, Hill's family members urged the two to turn themselves in.

Finally, after much prodding, they did, driving back to California and arriving at the Riverside County Sheriff's station on July 1, 1977.

When they walked in, they pointed to a wanted poster hanging on the station wall.

"We're them," said Hill.

"These were not two individuals who wanted to remain on the run," said Riverside County Sheriff Ben Clark.

Mother protests son's arrests

David Hill's mother, Edna, immediately came to her son's defense, and told reporters, "My David would do anything like that. I know the Lord's going to help. He'll take care of him."

Hill's father, J.W. Hill Sr., was not around to support the family. He hanged himself in 1948, leaving Edna to pick up the pieces of her broken life.

CHAPTER 7:
A confession brings horror to an end

Once in police custody, Kearney decided to make a full confession.

"He wanted to talk," Sett said. "For some reason or another, he wanted to talk. I was known as a pretty good interrogator, but Kearney really wanted to talk. He wanted to get this stuff off his chest."

His first order of business, however, was to exonerate his lover, Dave Hill, who Kearney claimed had no idea about the murders or the aftermath, since he hadn't been home and had no idea what dark secrets his longtime lover was keeping.

During that first 3 ½ hour session, Kearney said he committed the crimes when Hill was away, and only once had been forced to store the corpse of one of his victims in a closet for a few days to prevent Hill from catching him.

It's a scenario that seemed unlikely given the meticulous, time-consuming nature of Kearney's murders, which would have been very difficult to hide, and after Patrick Wayne Kearney started talking, both were arrested and held on $500,000 bonds.

Still, Kearney told reporters he would "plead guilty all the way" prior to his confession, likely in order to prevent implicating Hill, since there was a moratorium on California's death penalty at the time, and the most serious sentence he could receive would be life in prison.

Kearney made a full confession of his crimes, and during the first hours of interrogation admitted to a total of 28 murders, his victims between the ages of 5 and 28. He later copped to seven more.

After hearing Kearney's confession, "investigators surmised at this time that there are 15 workable cases. There are at least 13 additional cases that have been discussed by the suspects that may be involved also," said Ben Clark. "There are at least 28. There may be more, there may be less."

On some killings Kearney was vague, unable to remember names or his method of disposal. On others his memories were clear and highly detailed.

He talked about the victims whose names he didn't know, and gave sordid details about the ones whose names he did remember.

He told detectives Sett and Wilson that he committed his first murder while living in Culver City in 1962.

After shooting the man between the eyes, Kearney said, he dismembered and skinned the corpse. Then he decided to retrieve the bullet so it couldn't be traced to his gun. He used a hacksaw to access the slug.

Sett and Wilson learned that John LaMay had come over on March 13, 1977, to hang out with Hill, who wasn't home at the time. Kearney had invited the teen in to watch television to wait for his friend, then shot the teen in the back of his head. Later, he dismembered John's body, placing much of it in the trash bag and disposing any identifying features such as his head and hands in the desert.

The desert was Kearney's favorite dumping ground, for good reason.

"Things disappear very rapidly in the desert," he said. "You can put a small animal on an anthill and it disappears right in front of your eyes."

Preliminary hearings were set for July 15.

Boy's questions led to death

During questioning, Kearney also talked about Michael McGhee, and said that he hadn't intended to kill the boy.

Kearney told police that the camping trip was legit, or at least had been until the duo stopped at the place Kearney shared with Hill to pick up some of the supplies they'd need for the weekend.

According to Kearney, Michael McGhee was taking too much of an inventory of Kearney's possessions, which made the older man nervous, given the kid's arrest record.

"We were going to spend the weekend just outing and ... he kept talking about how he stole this guy's truck," Kearney told detectives in his confession. "And, then, when I got him in the house, he kept asking me, he said, 'Oh, you have all these things around,' you know, had all my radios and stuff, and he kept talking about, you know, 'You don't have any burglar alarms, do you? If you do, where are they?' You know, he kept asking very pertinent questions. I thought, 'Yeah, I made a mistake in befriending this kid. Letting him know where I live.' And I shot him before we ever went anywhere. Didn't go anywhere for the weekend."

Well, Kearney did, anyway. He cleaned up any evidence and disposed of what remained of Michael McGhee.

"I disposed of the body," he said. "You aren't going to find him."

Robert still lives with the overwhelming guilt of not have caught up with his brother to keep him from getting into Kearney's car.

"I just refused to believe it," said Robert, who used fantasy as a coping mechanism at the time of Michael's disappearance, and still does. "There was no body. There was no physical evidence.

I would rather think Michael's off in Mexico, goofing off, maybe on a beach somewhere."

Police hope for more answers

Kearney initially confessed to three murders, then upped the count to 10, leading officials to believe that many of their unsolved murders could be linked to the prolific Kearney.

They began asking pointed questions. Did he pick up Marines? Did he subdue his victims with booze and pills? Kearney stared at them blankly.

When Kearney was asked if he had ever inserted anything into the anuses of his victims, he shook his head indignantly and said, "I am not the Wooden Stake," unwilling to confess to anything that was not part of his routine.

(Serial killers are an interesting bunch. One of the other men trolling California's highways for victims, William Bonin, was also highly offended when he was linked to a murder that included that amputation of a young boy's penis. "I do not cut the dicks off little boys," Bonin said.)

Kearney did say that he used towels to prevent the blood from seeping through his floors as he dismembered the bodies."

At their arraignment on July 3, only Kearney responded when asked if he wanted a lawyer. He said, "Yes, I do." Hill was given a public defender.

A tour of death

After his confession, which had allowed police to close the books and several unsolved murders, Kearney then showed officers "six possible locations where he may have disposed of bodies," according to Clark.

Some had already been found, and Kearney was able to identify them for investigators.

Kearney then took police on a grim trek through five counties before reaching the arid desert where many of his sodomized, dismembered victims had been laid to uneasy rest.

Kearney took police to six sites near the California-Mexico border where, authorities said, "he may have disposed of bodies."

"He was pretty calm," said Imperial County Sheriff's Sergeant Lon Hettinger about Kearney's five-hour tour of the arid, isolated desert space he'd turned into a massive graveyard.

After a week, police had recovered 12 bodies.

The final body was unearthed from Kearney and Hill's former Culver City backyard, just behind the movie studio that once housed Desilu Productions.

"This appears to be the first of the murders," said Sheriff's Lt. Ed Douglas. "We believe this is the first residence in which they lived together."

Officials said the victim had been shot through the head.

First court appearance

On July 14, 1977, Patrick Kearney was formally indicted on two counts of murder, including the murder and mutilation of John LaMay.

By that date, Kearney had signed confessions to 28 murders, with twelve of the cases confirmed by police.

Kearney took full responsibility, and told police he killed because "it excited him and gave him a feeling of dominance."

The next day, because there was not enough evidence linking him to the crimes, a grand jury failed to indict David Hill, and charges against him were dismissed.

"The evidence against Mr. Hill was weak," said District Attorney Byron Morton, who dropped the charges against him and recommended his release.

Hill was driven away by his nephew, and under the advice of his attorney, never spoke about the case.

Kearney pleads guilty

On December 21, Patrick pled guilty to three counts of first-degree murder for the deaths of John LaMay, 17, Albert Rivera, 21, and Arturo Marquez, 24.

He was sentenced to life in prison.

But because there was a possibility that Kearney could at some point be paroled, police weren't done working the evidence they had against him.

"A number of filings with the district attorney is anticipated," said Sgt. Ted Toguchi. "Any information regarding specific crimes is premature and unfair to the parties involved."

While behind bars, Kearney penned numerous letters to police, gradually confessing to 18 more murders that he was prosecuted for and 11 more that police didn't have enough evidence to prosecute, bringing his total to 32 killings and ranking him among the ten most prolific serial killers in U.S. history.

"We had conversations with Kearney, and as a result of these conversations, we filed 17 counts of murder," said Sett.

Another count was added before the case went to court.

Questions will haunt police forever

Two weeks before he was sentenced in Los Angeles Superior Court for the 18 additional murders, Kearney met one last time with Sett, Wilson, Grossman and Los Angeles police Detective John St. John. The question they kept asking, and the one Kearney couldn't readily answer, was why?

It was, Kearney said, partly sexual gratification, partly fantasies, sometimes anger at his lover David Hill for running off so much. And, in one case, he killed out of sheer fear of getting caught, when he was sure the boy he'd picked up would tell his mother on him.

"I don't know if we'll ever know the total, because some bodies may be beyond recovery," said Lieutenant Edward Douglas of the Los Angeles Sheriff's Department.

He was charged with 18 more murders in February of 1978, including the first 12 victims Kearney had confessed to back in July.

On February 21, Kearney pled guilty to all 18 counts, and after having his guilty plea accepted, asked to be sentenced as quickly as possible.

Kearney – who told psychiatrists that "killing someone sounded sexually exciting" – clearly illustrated the need for the death penalty, said Municipal Court Judge Dickran Tevrizian, who accepted Kearney's guilty plea for the 18 new murders, then handed him over to a higher court for sentencing.

Because the crimes were committed before California reinstated the death penalty law in 1978, the maximum sentence Superior Court Paul Breckenridge Jr. could give him for the 21 murders was concurrent life sentences for all the crimes.

Kearney's attorney, had attempted to dissuade his client from pleading guilty – "I believe he has certain psychiatric defenses which is he refusing to let me raise," Jay Grossman said. "He didn't want to bring out certain facts in a jury trial. He was ashamed, I guess." – but Kearney wanted to bring the entire thing to an end as fast as possible.

"He wanted to be done quickly, so quickly that I don't think we even had the probation reports (usually reviewed by the court) when I sentenced him," Breckenridge said.

When he was again asked why, Kearney only offered a vague response.

"I prefer not to answer," he said. "I can't allow myself to think about it too much. It's too painful."

Breckenridge handed down the strongest sentence he could, which was 18 more life sentences, to run concurrently with the sentence he was already serving.

"It certainly appears the defendant is certainly deserving of whatever punishment the court can prescribe, and I would only hope that the Community Release Board will never see fit to parole Mr. Kearney because he appears to be an insult to humanity," Breckenridge said during the sentencing.

He has, Breckenridge added, "certainly perpetrated a series of ghastly, grisly and horrible crimes."

So far, the judge has gotten his wish. Kearney, now 75, continues to serve his life sentence at Mule Creek State Prison in Ione, California, located southeast of Sacramento.

And that's where he should stay, Sett said.

His victims remembered

According to various sources including the Department of Psychology at Radford University in Radford, Virginia, home to one of the country's top serial killer experts, Kearney's victims are as follows:

- John Doe, 19, killed in 1962
- John Doe, 16, killed in 1962
- Mike, 18, killed in 1962
- George, age unknown, killed in 1967
- John Demchik, 13, killed in 1971
- James Barwick, 17, date of death unknown
- Ronald Dean Smith Jr., 5, killed in 1974
- Albert Rivera, 21, killed in 1975
- Larry Gene Walters, 20, killed in 1975
- Robert "Billy" Bennefiel, 17, killed in 1976
- Kenneth Eugene Buchanan, 17, killed in 1976
- Oliver Peter Molitor, 13, killed in 1976
- Larry Armedariz, 15, killed in 1976
- Michael Craig McGhee, 13, killed in 1976
- Mark Andrew Orach, 20, killed in 1976
- Wilfred Lawrence Faherty, 30, killed in 1976
- Randall "Randy" Lawrence Moore, 26, killed in 1976
- David Allen, 27, killed in 1976
- Merle "Hondo" Chance, 8, killed in 1977
- John "Woody" Woods, 23, killed in 1977

- Larry Epsy, 17, date of death unknown
- Arturo Romos Marquez, 24, killed in 1977
- Nicholas "Nicky" Hernandez-Jimenez, 28, date of death unknown
- John Otis LaMay, 17, killed in 1977

CHAPTER 8:
Why necrophilia?

In 1979, Karen Greenlee was working as an apprentice embalmer at a funeral home in Sacramento, California, and tasked with driving the body of a 33-year-old man to his funeral. Instead, she disappeared for two days, and when they found her, they realized she'd been having sex with the week-dead man for 48 hours.

"Why do I do it? Why? Why? Fear of love, relationships. No romance ever hurt like this ... It's the pits. I'm a morgue rat. This is my rathole, perhaps my grave," she wrote in a letter she'd left in the grave before attempting to overdose on codeine.

She later confessed to having had sex with as many as 40 corpses, calling it her addiction.

While she was reticent to talk to the media, she did give an interview to the author of the book "Apocalypse Culture," where she spoke candidly about her desire to have sex with dead men.

"There are different aspects of sexual expression: touchy-feely, 69, even holding hands," she said. "That body is just lying there, but it has what it takes to make me happy. The cold, the aura of death, the smell of death, the funereal surroundings, it all contributes. I find the odor of death very erotic. There is also this attraction to blood. When you're on top of a body it tends to purge blood out of its mouth, while you're making passionate love.. You'd have to be there, I guess."

Well, yes, but preferably as the corpse, given the circumstances.

No chance for rejection

Most psychologists say that necrophilia is a way for people to attain sexual satisfaction without rejection, something Patrick Kearney was all too experienced with, despite his long relationship with David Hill.

While Greenlee's was considered regular necrophilia, Kearney took things a step further and committed necrophilic homicide, killing to obtain a corpse for sexual pleasure. (About 28 percent of people who suffer from necrophilia fall into this category. Almost all of the rest are situational necrophiliacs, and will land jobs where they have easy access to bodies, such as funeral homes or morgues.)

According to Drs. Jonathan Rosman and Phillip Resnick, the foremost authorities on necrophilia, there is also a category called necrophilic fantasy, which allows people with the disorder to imagine sex with a corpse without acting on their impulses.

For Kearney, killing gave him a sense of power, but by then having sex with the corpse he was able to accentuate the power and his feelings of self-esteem and self-worth because the dead could not reject him, no matter how they felt about him before he used his gun to take their lives.

For a man whose first sexual encounter was with the family dog, it should come as no surprise that Kearney took pleasure in the power of necrophilia.

Other known serial killers who practiced necrophilia include Ed Gein, who would masturbate using the genitalia he'd excised from corpses he'd stolen from area graves, Jeffrey Dahmer, Jerry Brudos, Ted Bundy, Dennis Nilsen, who only masturbated over the dead bodies, declaring them "too perfect and beautiful for the pathetic ritual of commonplace sex," Gary Ridgeway and Henry Lee Lucas, who said, "I like peace and quiet."

Edmund Kemper, who also used his victim's dead bodies to satisfy his sexual desires, said, "If I killed them, you know, they couldn't reject me as a man. It was more or less making a doll out of a human being... and carrying out my fantasies with a doll, a living human doll. I am sorry to sound so cold about this, but what I needed was to have a particular experience with a person, to possess them in the way I wanted to. I had to evict them from their bodies."

The hints people missed

According to an article appearing in Serial Killer Magazine, Kearney had a fondness for knives that he didn't do much to try and hide.

He regularly purchased butcher knives at a grocery store operated by Jerry Stevens.

He was, Stevens later told police, "a loner with an eerie sense of quiet about him."

Only Patrick Wayne Kearney knows how many he murdered, dismembered and dumped.

The Redondo Beach resident told police he began killing in 1962, then started his deadly once-a-month spree in 1974, preying mostly on hitchhikers, hustlers and street kids - one-third of them from the South Bay area.

Killer soon forgotten

Police probably relaxed a little with the Trash Bag Killer behind bars.

But here's the thing about serial killers.

As soon as one is captured and put away, another one — perhaps inspired by a sadist he's seen on the news or already on the prowl — is waiting in the wings to take their place.

In the United States alone, experts estimate that there are 40 to 50 serial killers operating at one time.

After Kearney came the Hillside Stranglers, followed by the capture of the Toolbox Killers Lawrence Bittaker and Roy Norris, who tortured teenage girls and forced them to pose for Polaroid photos before raping and murdering them, and Satanist Richard Ramirez, better known as the Night Stalker, who tortured and murdered 13 victims.

CHAPTER 9:
Parole becomes a nightmare for police and families

Because of the laws in place during the time Kearney was committing his crimes and was sentenced, he not only was unable to receive the death penalty – it did not exist at the time – the law also prevented him from being given consecutive life terms, which would have ensured that he stayed behind bars until death.

That means every six years, the detectives who heard his confession, the families who lost their children and siblings, must brace themselves to relive their nightmare, over and over again to ensure Kearney never has a chance to see the world again as a free man.

"I plan to contact as many of those families as I can," said Sheriff's Detective Al Sett, who served as lead investigator on the case before he retired. "I have a certain integrity about working homicides. I like to see killers in jail. That's where they belong. The mere thought this guy could get out. Who knows what a parole board will do after three times?"

Elizabeth McGhee, who didn't realize her brother had driven off with Kearney until it was much too late, said, "We just always presumed he'd be in prison for more than 100 years."

"This guy's a killer, a serial killer," said sheriff's homicide Detective Louis Danoff. "He's got a master's degree in murder. We're trying to alert people about him to keep him where he is. One of our concerns is, people have forgotten about him."

Family continues to fight against parole

Robert Bennefiel's sister feels as though she has been fighting to keep Patrick Wayne Kearney behind bars for most of her life, a process that insists on unearthing the pain that began the day she, her brother and her parents learned that their brother was a victim of one of California's most heinous criminals.

Initially they believed the 18-year-old student at Torrance, California's Aviation High School had run away, and so did police, until a neighbor read a newspaper article about Kearney, and realized the missing man was Kearney's type.

"Police took a picture to Kearney in 1981, and asked, 'Is this one of your victims?'" Born said. "Kearney identified him. To this day it eats my other brother up that the picture he took out of his wallet was the one that slime looked at."

Kearney said he'd dumped Bennefiel's body in a landfill; his remains have never been found.

In some way, the lack of a body gives Born a bit of comfort.

"I don't know if it's doubt or hope," she said. "We don't have a body. Kearney didn't know my brother's name. There's always that little bit in your mind. For so many years, you see someone who looks like him, you take a double take, even to this day. We moved on. "But it's always in your head. It doesn't go away. There's always going to be anger and bitterness. I mean, my God, he killed my brother!"

Michael McGhee's sister also continues to fight to keep Kearney behind bars.

"I want to let them know the slime he is," she said. "I want to tell them how he affected people's lives. He needs to account for what he's done. He took my naivete away. Before this happened, I used to go down to the beach at night and walk along the ocean. But he took that away. I realized I couldn't do that anymore. There were a lot of things I wouldn't do anymore. It wasn't safe. I realized how sick the world is."

For families of the victims, the case never stops. Not as long as Kearney lives. Not as long as he pleads for parole.

"That son of a bitch," said Stephen Demchik, who desperately misses his son, John. "That son of a bitch."

CHAPTER 10:
Confession recanted

In 1981, Patrick Kearney wrote a letter to the Riverside Press-Enterprise recanting his confession, four years after he pleaded guilty to the murders of 21 young men and boys in and around Redondo Beach.

"I have another tidbit of news for you," Kearney wrote. "I didn't kill anybody. That's all I'll say at the moment."

In his retraction, he asked to be released from Soledad Prison, where he at the time was serving out his two life sentences.

It was the second petition for release from prison. A month earlier, he had asked Riverside Superior Court to release him, in part because he did not commit the grisly murders, but also because he felt he was unfairly advised by his defense attorney.

"The person in custody pleaded guilty to felonies which he did not commit," Kearney said. "The pleas were given due to threats and other forms of duress."

It's unlikely he'll ever get out of prison, though, given the nature of his crimes.

Deputy District Attorney Diane Vezzani puts Kearney's chances of ever being released "between slim and none because of the horrible nature of the offenses themselves," she told one regional newspaper.

Further cementing his life sentence is his unwillingness to attend his parole hearings, which disappoints Vezzani tremendously, since he does not have to face the friends and families of his victims once every six years, although they attend to ensure that his concurrent sentencing terms don't somehow allow him the freedom to kill again.

"I'd like to tell him, 'Big man. What a big man you are,'" Vezzani said. "'Had to use a gun to have your way with little boys. What a big, brave man.'"

She's not the only one who attends Kearney's parole hearings religiously.

"It's critical that we testify at his (parole) hearing to make sure we keep him where he belongs," said detective Al Sett, who sat through Kearney's grueling 3 ½-hour confession. "This guy's a killer. A brilliant mind. My fear is if he gets out, he won't make the same mistakes again. And we'd never catch him."

Family struggles to rebuild

JoAnn O'Conner, whose 5-year-old son Ronald Dean Smith was among Kearney's victims, isn't interested in facing the man who robbed her of a lifetime with her son. Instead, she writes letters to the parole board expressing her desire to keep Kearney behind bars.

"I've already gone through the mourning and healing from the anger. I don't think it'd be good for me to attend," she said. "It's like dead flesh. You don't bring it up because it stinks."

Still, not a day passes that the family doesn't think about the youngest member of their family.

"Ronnie was the baby of the family, and there's not a holiday or day that goes by that we don't imagine what he'd be doing, what he'd look like now," said his aunt, Ronnie Jewette. "His death was so terrible and it made me afraid to let my own children go out anymore. When Ronnie died, we all learned you can't be too trusting. His death changed everything, everyone."

As for his mom, O'Conner clings to the precious memories she carried of her only child.

"I can still smell what his skin smelled like and how his hair felt and, when I close my eyes, I hear his voice," O'Conner told the Daily Breeze, the newspaper that covers Los Angeles County's

South Bay area and was busy during the period of time when the Trash Bag Killer was on the prowl.

"Your life is never the same after something like that," she added. "My life went through radical changes. I changed everything in my life. If I were going to survive it, I had to make some changes."

The family celebrates Ronnie's birthday, pulling out the collection of photographs they have of the boy and sharing their favorite memories, even through their tears.

"All the family has pictures out now and we talk about Ronnie freely," his mother said. "It's nice to be able to put those pictures out and share those happy memories."

A life behind bars

Kearney is currently incarcerated at Mule Creek State Prison in Ione, California, where he was moved in 2014.

Kearney's allowed to attend college equivalency classes, but has a cell to himself and is confined mostly to it.

"He's in a protective housing unit like some of the others," said prison Sgt. Tony Diaz. "Otherwise, their safety would be jeopardized. This keeps him away from others who might want to do him harm. And it keeps him away from those he might want to hurt."

He, like many serial killers, gets letters, including one from a woman in Wisconsin. When he wrote back, he said, "Thanks for writing. So what's it like there in the North Pole? Thanks for the photo. I like your hair."

His famous fellow inmates there include Lyle Menendez, one of two brothers who killed their parents in 1989; Andrew Luster, heir to the Max Factor fortune who chose to use GBH to sexually assault numerous women in 2003; Robert John Bardo, who murdered "My Sister Sam" actress Rebecca Schaeffer in 1989 after stalking her for three years; mass murderer and religious fanatic John Linley Frazier; Michael Carson, who along with his wife, Suzanne, murdered three people; Charles Manson as well as Manson follower Charles "Tex" Watson; Death Row Records founder Suge Knight; and serial killer Herbert Mullin, who liked to sing, often, which offended his former cell neighbor William Bonin, who was executed in 1996.

CHAPTER 11:
A survivor tells his story

As a child, Tony Stewart used to mow lawns for Patrick Kearney to make extra money.

One of seven kids, Stewart came from a poor family and the landlord of their Redondo Beach home helped the children make extra money by not only giving them jobs around his property, but also helping them line up other work.

Stewart remembers being introduced to Kearney and landing the job of mowing his lawn, which he did for about four years.

Years later, their paths would cross again, and it would be a meeting that Stewart would never forget.

"I was 19 years old and fresh out of high school," he said. "The only thought on my mind besides searching for beautiful women, playing guitar and surfing waves, was to attend as many wild parties as possible with my friends."

It was the free-spirited 1970s, and Stewart's life was carefree.

He'd had a car his dad had given him for graduation, a 1964 Chevy Impala convertible that was perfect for cruising along the Pacific Highway, but the engine quickly gave out, forcing Stewart to hitchhike when he couldn't catch a ride with friends.

One night in April, after a day of surfing and skateboarding, Stewart was planning to hitchhike the five miles home, but first stopped at a local convenience store hoping that he could talk someone into buying him some beer.

After his mission failed, he headed for the highway and stuck out his thumb.

He was surprised when a familiar face in a pickup truck pulled over to offer the ride.

"You're Patrick," Stewart recalled. "I used to mow your yard."

After the usual chitchat between people who hadn't seen one another in years, Stewart told Kearney that he was hoping to find someone to buy him a quart of beer, and Kearney volunteered, with one caveat.

"You'll have to drink it at my house. You're a minor and I don't want you getting in any trouble," Kearney said.

It was about midnight when they got to Kearney's Redondo Beach home – "the same house where I mowed his grass and did yard work for four years, earning $3.00 each time I worked for him," Stewart recalled.

Kearney told Stewart to sit down, and the older man went into the kitchen, asking Stewart about his life as a free-spirited California teen while rustling through silverware.

When Kearney came back, things got strange.

"He reached into a black doctor's type bag beside the television and pulled out a stethoscope. He put it around his neck and said, 'I used to be a doctor,' then asked if he could listen to my heartbeat, adding that he wanted to hear if my heart slowed down while I'm drinking. I was so naïve, I calmly said, 'Sure, I don't care.' I didn't think anything odd about the request," Stewart said. "Besides, I figured, he did buy me beer. He placed the instrument on my chest outside my shirt and began moving it around trying to locate my heart. Next, he asked, 'Could you lift up your shirt? I can't hear anything.' Without thinking, I lifted it up for him. He continued to move it around on my chest.

"Suddenly, he began to slowly lower the hearing mechanism towards my belly button. I did not feel comfortable with this and told him I need to get going. I added that my parents might lock me out if I'm out too late. As I spoke, I heard someone keying the doorknob to enter the residence, about to enter. Kearney's face quickly turned to the direction of the sound. It was his roommate, David Hill. As Hill began to open the front door, Kearney quickly jumped back away from me, as if he didn't want his roommate to know what he was doing.

Nervously, he said, 'Dave, do you remember Tony? He used to mow our yard. Say hello.' Dave Hill quietly said 'hi' and continued walking straight to the bedroom. As he was walking, I repeated, 'Well, I really have to get going.' I wanted to make sure Hill heard me. Pat said 'OK, let me get the keys to my truck.' I heard him tell Hill, 'David, I will be right back, I'm just going to drive Tony home.'"

According to Stewart, Kearney said very little on the way home, so he filled the truck with conversation, thanking him for the beer, telling him how great it had been to see him again after so much time and they should do it again soon.

When they got close to a park near Stewart's home, he told Kearney he could pull over, since his house was just across the street, lying about the true location of his home because of Kearney's strange behavior.

Kearney took Stewart's earlier words to heart, and made him promise to stop to visit some more the next day.

"I remember Pat Kearney had a strange look in his eyes that I will never forget. It was almost hypnotic. He mentioned how good it was to see me again and he looked forward to tomorrow. I said, 'Well I'd better go,' and then I began walking north. I looked back and watched as he turned the truck around and began driving away. Then I ran full speed around the corner toward my house. I looked over my shoulder and noticed him turning around again. He must have seen me running because he made a U-turn in my direction. I made it to a house around the corner and hid behind my fence. I watched him slowing drive by, looking around, but he didn't see me. I thought it was strange that he turned around. I wouldn't realize it until months later, that if his roommate hadn't come home when he did, I might have been killed," Stewart said.

Months later, Stewart was hanging out at a girlfriend's house when his brother called him and told him to turn on the news.

"I did, and almost went into shock at what I saw," Stewart said. "It was Patrick's face on the television and they were saying that he killed thirty-two people, including young boys. I almost fainted. I began to tremble, thinking about the night I was at his house alone drinking beer, and how he acted. I thought, 'My God, I was alone with a serial killer drinking beer in the middle of the night.' I had nightmares for weeks after that evening, reliving that night over and over in my head."

Another's last moments recalled

That late night beer would not be the only encounter Stewart would have with Kearney, although his second would be a vicarious one.

He and his friend Gene Austin – the proud owner of a red Ford van with chrome wheels – were going to a party that promised to be the biggest blow-out of the summer.

Austin described it as "the party of all parties" as they headed to the event, along with their mutual friend, Billy, and one of Gene's friends, John Woods, who went by the nickname Woody.

Woody, a tall redhead who Stewart said reminded him of Art Garfunkel, was talking about Vietnam, telling gruesome stories of wartime while they cruised around drinking a few beers, waiting for the party to get started.

The party turned out to be as much of a bust as their pre-party conversations.

By the time they arrived, the cops had already been called, and were ordering everyone to leave.

The foursome drove around drinking a few more beers, then dropped Woody off at a bar and Billy at home.

Tony decided to stay at Gene's house overnight so the two could go surfing the next morning.

When the surf report revealed a lack of surf-worthy waves they decided to wash Gene's van.

As they were working, detectives arrived with guns pointed at the two teens, and ordered them away from the van and onto the ground.

The two had no idea what was going on, until one of the detectives asked them why they were washing the blood out of the van.

Horrified, Tony and Gene then learned that Woody had been found earlier that morning in San Diego, shot in the head.

Since San Diego was about two hours away from the bar where they had dropped Woody off the night before, the two assumed the Art Garfunkel lookalike had met someone at the bar and had been offered a ride that ended up turning deadly.

Later, when the names of Patrick Kearney's victims were released, it included John Woods.

Notable:

A tracing of Patrick Wayne Kearney's hand is available for sale on the internet via a site that specializes in macabre merchandise. Kearney signed the item eight times in six different languages, including Roman, Gregg Shorthand, Arabic, Cyrillic, Hiragana and Katakana. It is $55.

According to letters to pen pals, Patrick Kearney's obsessive interest in other serial killers hasn't waned behind bars. He wrote asking about Ian Brady, a Scottish serial killer who murdered multiple children in the 1960s with his girlfriend, Myra Hindley, whom he'd brainwashed into becoming his slave.

Conclusion

Every six years, Patrick Kearney will be up for parole, and every six years, a police officer or family member will fight it.

The man with so much anger from a troubled childhood is unlikely to be able to control his desire for revenge if released, and the Mule Creek parole board is unlikely to take the risk.

But just as stopping Randy Kraft and William Bonin – the men who for a time shared the nickname the Freeway Killer with Patrick Kearney because they used the California freeway system to procure their human playthings – there's always another one waiting in the wings, another angry man seeking vengeance for some sort of childhood horror.

Hopefully they don't move in next door.

GET ONE OF MY AUDIOBOOKS FOR FREE

audible
an amazon company

If you haven't joined Audible yet, you can get any of my audiobooks for FREE!
Go to www.JackRosewood.com to find out more!

More books by Jack Rosewood

Among the annals of American serial killers, few were as complex and prolific as Joseph Paul Franklin. At a gangly 5'11, Franklin hardly looked imposing, but once he put a rifle in his hands and an interracial couple in his cross hairs, Joseph Paul Franklin was as deadly as any serial killer. In this true crime story you will learn about how one man turned his hatred into a vocation of murder, which eventually left over twenty people dead across America. Truly, Franklin's story is not only that of a true crime serial killer, but also one of racism in America as he chose Jews, blacks, and especially interracial couples as his victims.

Joseph Paul Franklin's story is unique among serial killers biographies because he gained no sexual satisfaction from his murders and there is no indication that he was ever compelled to kill. But make no mistake about it, by all definitions; Joseph Paul Franklin was a serial killer. In fact, the FBI stated that Franklin was the first known racially motivated serial killer in the United States: he planned to kill as many of his perceived enemies as possible in order to start an epic race war across the country. An examination of Franklin's life will reveal how he became a racially motivated serial killer and the steps he took to carry out his one man war against the world.

Open the pages of this e-book to read a disturbing story of true crime murder in America's heartland. You will be disturbed and perplexed at Franklin's murderous campaign as he made himself a one man death squad, eliminating as many of his political enemies that he could. But you will also be captivated with Franklin's shrewdness and cunning as he avoided the authorities for years while he carried out his diabolical plot!

THE YOSEMITE PARK KILLER

While some would say that American serial killer Cary Stayner was influenced by family tragedy – his already-troubled family was shattered when his brother was abducted for seven years and held as a sex slave before his heroic return inspired the miniseries "I Know My First Name Is Steven" – in reality, Cary Stayner's true crime story is much more ominous.

The handsome, outdoorsy guy with a love for marijuana, nude beaches and the Sierra Nevada mountain range where he once spotted Bigfoot had been harboring fantasies of brutally killing women years before his brother's abduction turned the Stayner family upside down.

And in the annals of historical serial killers, Stayner's story stands out, because for months he made one of the most beautiful places on earth a nightmare for women when California's majestic Yosemite National Park became his own devil's playground, and he finally found himself unable to control his long-suppressed urges.

Because he didn't look menacing, the man one FBI agent compared to actor Tom Laughlin in "Billy Jack" was able to gain the trust of his victims, and three vacationing women who were staying at the lodge where he lived and worked during the busy tourist season and a nature-loving teacher who help kids become stewards of the land she loved made that fatal mistake before they were savagely, sadistically murdered.

The biography of serial killer Cary Stayner and his psychopathic crime spree leaves spine-tingling chills, because as far as the outside world was concerned, he was a fairly normal guy who found himself uncontrollably compelled to kill.

Stayner has been on death row in California's famed San Quentin for more than 10 years, but for the families of his victims, no punishment is just enough to make up for the vibrant lives Stayner took, making him one of the most depraved American serial killers in contemporary history.

In the world of American serial killers, few can beat Donald Henry "Peewee" Gaskins when it comes to depravity, cunning, and quite possibly the sheer number of murders. Do not let the nickname "Peewee" fool you, if someone did not take Gaskins seriously, then that person usually ended up dead! In this true crime book about an infamous serial killer, you will delve into the mind of a truly twisted man who claimed scores of victims from the 1950s until 1982, which made him the most prolific serial killer in South Carolina history and quite possibly in all of American history!

Criminal profiling has helped law enforcement capture a number of serial killers throughout history and has also aided mental health professionals understand some of the motives behind their dastardly deeds, but in many ways Gaskins defied most profiles. The range of Gaskins' victims was only equaled by the plethora of reasons he chose to kill: many of the murders were done to appease Gaskins' unnatural carnal desires, while other victims lost their lives during his career as a contract killer. Truly, in the twisted world of psychopaths and sociopaths Gaskins is definitely in the top tier – he was a predator among predators.

Many of the details of Gaskins' life will shock you and still other things will make you horrified by his inhumanity, but in the end you will find that it is impossible to put down this captivating read! So open the book and your mind to see what you will learn in this truly unique serial killer's biography.

This is the true story of the "Meanest Man In America", Donald Henry Gaskins.

GET THESE BOOKS FOR FREE

Go to www.jackrosewood.com

and get these E-Books for free!

FREE BONUS CHAPTER

The making of a serial killer

"I was born with the devil in me," said H.H. Holmes, who in 1893 took advantage of the World's Fair – and the extra room he rented out in his Chicago mansion – to kill at least 27 people without attracting much attention.

"I could not help the fact that I was a murderer, no more than the poet can help the inspiration to sing. I was born with the evil one standing as my sponsor beside the bed where I was ushered into the world, and he has been with me since," Holmes said.

The idea of "I can't help it" is one of the hallmarks of many serial killers, along with an unwillingness to accept responsibility for their actions and a refusal to acknowledge that they themselves used free will to do their dreadful deeds.

"Yes, I did it, but I'm a sick man and can't be judged by the standards of other men," said Juan Corona, who killed 25 migrant workers in California in the late 1960s and early 1970s, burying them in the very fruit orchards where they'd hoped to build a better life for their families.

Dennis Rader, who called himself the BTK Killer (Bind, Torture, Kill) also blamed some unknown facet to his personality, something he called Factor X, for his casual ability to kill one family, then go home to his own, where he was a devoted family man.

"When this monster entered my brain, I will never know, but it is here to stay. How does one cure himself? I can't stop it, the monster goes on, and hurts me as well as society. Maybe you can stop him. I can't," said Rader, who said he realized he was different than the other kids before he entered high school. "I actually think I may be possessed with demons."

But again, he blamed others for not stopping him from making his first murderous move.

"You know, at some point in time, someone should have picked something up from me and identified it," he later said.

Rader was not the only serial killer to place the blame far away from himself.

William Bonin actually took offense when a judge called him "sadistic and guilty of monstrous criminal conduct."

"I don't think he had any right to say that to me," Bonin later whined. "I couldn't help myself. It's not my fault I killed those boys."

It leaves us always asking why

For those of us who are not serial killers, the questions of why and how almost always come to mind, so ill equipped are we to understand the concept of murder on such a vast scale.

"Some nights I'd lie awake asking myself, 'Who the hell is this BTK?'" said FBI profiler John Douglas, who worked the Behavioral Science Unit at Quantico before writing several best-selling books, including "Mindhunter: Inside the FBI's Elite Serial Crime Unit," and "Obsession: The FBI's Legendary Profiler Probes the Psyches of Killers, Rapists, and Stalkers and Their Victims and Tells How to Fight Back."

The questions were never far from his mind - "What makes a guy like this do what he does? What makes him tick?" – and it's the kind of thing that keeps profilers and police up at night, worrying, wondering and waiting for answers that are not always so easily forthcoming.

Another leader into the study of madmen, the late FBI profiler Robert Ressler - who coined the terms serial killer as well as criminal profiling – also spent sleepless nights trying to piece together a portrait of many a killer, something that psychiatrist James Brussel did almost unfailingly well in 1940, when a pipe bomb killer enraged at Con Edison was terrorizing New York City.

(Brussel told police what the killer would be wearing when they arrested him, and although he was caught at home late at night, wearing his pajamas, when police asked him to dress, he emerged from his room wearing a double-breasted suit, exactly as Brussel had predicted.)

"What is this force that takes a hold of a person and pushes them over the edge?" wondered Ressler, who interviewed scores of killers over the course of his illustrious career.

In an effort to infiltrate the minds of serial killers, Douglas and Ressler embarked on a mission to interview some of the most deranged serial killers in the country, starting their journey in California, which "has always had more than its share of weird and spectacular crimes," Douglas said.

In their search for a pattern, they determined that there are essential two types of serial killers: organized and disorganized.

Organized killers

Organized killers were revealed through their crime scenes, which were neat, controlled and meticulous, with effort taken both in the crime and with their victims. Organized killers also take care to leave behind few clues once they're done.

Dean Corll was an organized serial killer. He tortured his victims overnight, carefully collecting blood and bodily fluids on a sheet of plastic before rolling them up and burying them and their possessions, most beneath the floor of a boat shed he'd rented, going there late at night under the cover of darkness.

Disorganized killers

On the flip side of the coin, disorganized killers grab their victims indiscriminately, or act on the spur of the moment, allowing victims to collect evidence beneath their fingernails when they fight back and oftentimes leaving behind numerous clues including weapons.

"The disorganized killer has no idea of, or interest in, the personalities of his victims," Ressler wrote in his book "Whoever Fights Monsters," one of several detailing his work as a criminal profiler. "He does not want to know who they are, and many times takes steps to obliterate their personalities by quickly knocking them unconscious or covering their faces or otherwise disfiguring them."

Cary Stayner – also known as the Yosemite Killer – became a disorganized killer during his last murder, which occurred on the fly when he was unable to resist a pretty park educator.

Lucky for other young women in the picturesque park, he left behind a wide range of clues, including four unmatched tire tracks from his aging 1979 International Scout.

"The crime scene is presumed to reflect the murderer's behavior and personality in much the same way as furnishings reveal the homeowner's character," Douglas and Ressler later wrote, expanding on their findings as they continued their interview sessions.

Serial killers think they're unique – but they're not

Dr. Helen Morrison — a longtime fixture in the study of serial killers who keeps clown killer John Wayne Gacy's brain in her basement (after Gacy's execution she sent the brain away for an analysis that proved it to be completely normal) — said that at their core, most serial killers are essentially the same.

While psychologists still haven't determined the motives behind what drives serial killers to murder, there are certain characteristics they have in common, said Morrison, who has studied or interviewed scores of serial killers and wrote about her experiences in "My Life Among the Serial Killers."

Most often men, serial killers tend to be talkative hypochondriacs who develop a remorseless addiction to the brutality of murder.

Too, they are able to see their victims as inanimate objects, playthings, of you will, around simply for their amusement.

Empathy? Not on your life.

"They have no appreciation for the absolute agony and terror and fear that the victim is demonstrating," said Morrison. "They just see the object in front of them. A serial murderer has no feelings. Serial killers have no motives. They kill only to kill an object."

In doing so, they satisfy their urges, and quiet the tumultuous turmoil inside of them.

"You say to yourself, 'How could anybody do this to another human being?'" Morrison said. "Then you realize they don't see them as humans. To them, it's like pulling the wings off a fly or the legs off a daddy longlegs.... You just want to see what happens. It's the most base experiment."

Nature vs. nurture?

For many serial killers, the desire to kill is as innate at their hair or eye color, and out of control, but most experts say that childhood trauma is an experience shared by them all.

In 1990, Colin Wilson and Donald Seaman conducted a study of serial killers behind bars and found that childhood problems were the most influential factors that led serial killers down their particular path of death and destruction.

Former FBI profiler Robert Ressler – who coined the terms serial killer and criminal profiling – goes so far as to say that 100 percent of all serial killers experienced childhoods that were not filled with happy memories of camping trips or fishing on the lake.

According to Ressler, of all the serial killers he interviewed or studied, each had suffered some form of abuse as a child - either sexual, physical or emotional abuse, neglect or rejection by parents or humiliation, including instances that occurred at school.

For those who are already hovering psychologically on edge due to unfortunate genetics, such events become focal points that drive a killer to act on seemingly insane instincts.

Because there is often no solid family unit – parents are missing or more focused on drugs and alcohol, sexual abuse goes unnoticed, physical abuse is commonplace – the child's development becomes stunted, and they can either develop deep-seeded rage or create for themselves a fantasy world where everything is perfect, and they are essentially the kings of their self-made castle.

That was the world of Jeffrey Dahmer, who recognized his need for control much later, after hours spent in analysis where he learned the impact of a sexual assault as a child as well as his parents' messy, rage-filled divorce.

"After I left the home, that's when I started wanting to create my own little world, where I was the one who had complete control," Dahmer said. "I just took it way too far."

Dahmer's experiences suggest that psychopathic behavior likely develops in childhood, when due to neglect and abuse, children revert to a place of fantasy, a world where the victimization of the child shifts toward others.

"The child becomes sociopathic because the normal development of the concepts of right and wrong and empathy towards others is retarded because the child's emotional and social development occurs within his self-centered fantasies. A person can do no wrong in his own world and the pain of others is of no consequence when the purpose of the fantasy world is to satisfy the needs of one person," according to one expert.

As the lines between fantasy and reality become blurred, fantasies that on their own are harmless become real, and monsters like Dean Corll find themselves strapping young boys down to a wooden board, raping them, torturing them and listening to them scream, treating the act like little more than a dissociative art project that ends in murder.

Going inside the mind: Psychopathy and other mental illnesses

While not all psychopaths are serial killers – many compulsive killers do feel some sense of remorse, such as Green River Killer Gary Ridgeway did when he cried in court after one victim's father offered Ridgeway his forgiveness – those who are, Morrison said, are unable to feel a speck of empathy for their victims.

Their focus is entirely on themselves and the power they are able to assert over others, especially so in the case of a psychopath.

Psychopaths are charming — think Ted Bundy, who had no trouble luring young women into his car by eliciting sympathy with a faked injury — and have the skills to easily manipulate their victims, or in some cases, their accomplices.

Dean Corll was called a Svengali — a name taken from a fictional character in George du Maurier's 1895 novel "Trilby" who seduces, dominates and exploits the main character, a young girl — for being able to enlist the help of several neighborhood boys who procured his youthful male victims without remorse, even when the teens were their friends.

Some specific traits of serial killers, determined through years of profiling, include:

- **Smooth talking but insincere.** Ted Bundy was a charmer, the kind of guy that made it easy for people to be swept into his web. "I liked him immediately, but people like Ted can fool you completely," said Ann Rule, author of the best-selling "Stranger Beside Me," about her experiences with Bundy, a man she considered a friend. "I'd been a cop, had all that psychology — but his mask was perfect. I say that long acquaintance can help you know someone. But you can never be really sure. Scary."
- **Egocentric and grandiose.** Jack the Ripper thought the world of himself, and felt he would outsmart police, so much so that he sent letters taunting the London

officers. "Dear Boss," he wrote, "I keep on hearing the police have caught me but they won't fix me just yet. I have laughed when they look so clever and talk about being on the right track. That joke about Leather Apron gave me real fits. I am down on whores and I shan't quit ripping them till I do get buckled. Grand work the last job was. I gave the lady no time to squeal. How can they catch me now? I love my work and want to start again. You will soon hear of me with my funny little games. I saved some of the proper red stuff in a ginger beer bottle over the last job to write with but it went thick like glue and I can't use it. Red ink is fit enough I hope ha. ha. The next job I do I shall clip the lady's ears off and send to the police officers ... My knife's so nice and sharp I want to get to work right away if I get a chance. Good luck."

- **Lack of remorse or guilt.** Joel Rifkin was filled with self-pity after he was convicted of killing and dismembering at least nine women. He called his conviction a tragedy, but later, in prison, he got into an argument with mass murderer Colin Ferguson over whose killing spree was more important, and when Ferguson taunted him for only killing women, Rifkin said, "Yeah, but I had more victims."

- **Lack of empathy.** Andrei Chikatilo, who feasted on bits of genitalia both male and female after his kills, thought nothing of taking a life, no matter how torturous it was for his victims. "The whole thing - the cries, the blood, the agony - gave me relaxation and a certain pleasure," he said.

- **Deceitful and manipulative.** John Wayne Gacy refused to take responsibility for the 28 boys buried beneath his house, even though he also once said that clowns can get away with murder. "I think after 14 years under truth serum had I committed the crime I would have known it," said the man the neighbors all claimed to like. "There's got to be something that would... would click in my mind. I've had photos of 21 of the victims and I've looked at them all over the years here and I've never recognized anyone of them."

- **Shallow emotions.** German serial killer Rudolph Pliel, convicted of killing 10 people and later took his own life in prison, compared his "hobby" of murder to playing cards, and later told police, "What I did is not such a great harm, with all these surplus women nowadays. Anyway, I had a good time."

- **Impulsive.** Tommy Lynn Sells, who claimed responsibility for dozens of murders throughout the Midwest and South, saw a woman at a convenience store and followed her home, an impulse he was unable to control. He waited until the house went dark, then "I went into this house. I go to the first bedroom I see...I don't know whose room it is and, and, and, and I start stabbing." The victim was the woman's young son.

- **Poor behavior controls**. "I wished I could stop but I could not. I had no other thrill or happiness," said UK killer Dennis Nilsen, who killed at least 12 young men via strangulation, then bathed and dressed their bodies before disposing of them, often by burning them.

- **Need for excitement.** For Albert Fish - a masochistic killer with a side of sadism that included sending a letter to the mother of one of his victims, describing in detail how he cut, cooked and ate her daughter - even the idea of his own death was one he found particularly thrilling. "Going to the electric chair will be the supreme thrill of my life," he said.

- **Lack of responsibility.** "I see myself more as a victim rather than a perpetrator," said Gacy, in a rare moment of admitting the murders. "I was cheated out of my childhood. I should never have been convicted of anything more serious than running a cemetery without a license. They were just a bunch of worthless little queers and punks."

- **Early behavior problems.** "When I was a boy I never had a friend in the world," said German serial killer

Heinrich Pommerencke, who began raping and murdering girls as a teen.

- **Adult antisocial behavior.** Gary Ridgeway pleaded guilty to killing 48 women, mostly prostitutes, who were easy prey and were rarely reported missing – at least not immediately. "I don't believe in man, God nor Devil. I hate the whole damned human race, including myself... I preyed upon the weak, the harmless and the unsuspecting. This lesson I was taught by others: Might makes right."

'I felt like it'

Many psychopaths will say after a crime, "I did it because I felt like it," with a certain element of pride.

That's how BTK killer Dennis Rader felt, and because he had no sense of wrong regarding his actions, he was able to carry on with his normal life with his wife and children with ease.

Someone else's demeanor might have changed, they may have become jittery or anxious, and they would have been caught.

Many serial killers are so cold they are can pop into a diner right after a murder, never showing a sign of what they've done.

"Serial murderers often seem normal," according to the FBI. "They have families and/or a steady job."

"They're so completely ordinary," Morrison added. "That's what gets a lot of victims in trouble."

That normalcy is often what allows perpetrators to get away with their crimes for so long.

Unlike mass murderers such as terrorists who generally drop off the radar before perpetrating their event, serial killers blend in. They might seem a bit strange – neighbors noticed that Ed Gein wasn't too big on personal hygiene, and neighbors did think it was odd that William Bonin hung out with such young boys - but not so much so that anyone would ask too many questions.

"That's why so many people often say, "I had no idea" or "He was such a nice guy" after a friend or neighbor is arrested.

And it's also why people are so very, very stunned when they see stories of serial killers dominating the news.

"For a person with a conscience, Rader's crimes seem hideous, but from his point of view, these are his greatest accomplishments and he is anxious to share all of the wonderful things he has done," said Jack Levin, PhD, director of the Brudnick Center on Violence and Conflict at Northeastern University in Boston and the author of "Extreme Killings."

A new take on psychopathy

Psychopathy is now diagnosed as antisocial personality disorder, a prettier spin on an absolutely horrifying diagnosis.

According to studies, almost 50 percent of men in prison and 21 percent of women in prison have been diagnosed with antisocial personality disorder.

Of serial killers, Ted Bundy (who enjoyed sex with his dead victims), John Wayne Gacy and Charles Manson (who encouraged others to do his dirty work which included the murder of pregnant Sharon Tate) were all diagnosed with this particular affliction, which allowed them to carry out their crimes with total disregard toward others or toward the law.

They showed no remorse.

Schizophrenia

Many known serial killers were later diagnosed with some other form of mental illness, including schizophrenia, believed to be behind the crimes of David Berkowitz (he said his neighbor's dog told him to kill his six victims in the 1970s), Ed Gein, whose grisly saving of skin, bones and various female sex parts was a desperate effort to resurrect his death mother and Richard Chase (the vampire of Sacramento, who killed six people in California in order to drink their blood).

Schizophrenia includes a wide range of symptoms, ranging from hallucinations and delusions to living in a catatonic state.

Borderline personality disorder

Borderline personality disorder – which is characterized by intense mood swings, problems with interpersonal relationships and impulsive behaviors – is also common in serial killers.

Some diagnosed cases of borderline personality disorder include Aileen Wuornos, a woman whose horrific childhood and numerous sexual assaults led her to murder one of her rapists, after which she spiraled out of control and killed six other men who picked her up along with highway in Florida, nurse Kristen H. Gilbert, who killed four patients at a Virginia hospital with overdoses of epinephrine, and Dahmer, whose murder count rose to 17 before he was caught.

With a stigma still quite present regarding mental illness, it's likely we will continue to diagnose serial killers and mass murderers after the fact, too late to protect their victims.

Top signs of a serial killer

While there is still no simple thread of similarities – which is why police and the FBI have more trouble in real life solving crimes than they do on shows like "Criminal Minds" – there are some things to look for, experts say.

- **Antisocial Behavior.** Psychopaths tend to be loners, so if a child that was once gregarious and outgoing becomes shy and antisocial, this could be an issue. Jeffrey Dahmer was a social, lively child until his parents moved to Ohio for his father's new job. There, he regressed – allegedly after being sexually molested – and began focusing his attentions on dissecting road kill rather than developing friendships.

- **Arson.** Fire is power, and power and control are part of the appeal for serial killers, who enjoy having their victims at their mercy. David Berkowitz was a pyromaniac as a child – his classmates called him Pyro as a nickname, so well-known was he for his fire obsession - and he reportedly started more than 1,000 fires in New York before he became the Son of Sam killer.

- **Torturing animals.** Serial killers often start young, and test boundaries with animals including family or neighborhood pets. According to studies, 70 percent of violent offenders have episodes of animal abuse in their childhood histories, compared to just 6 percent of nonviolent offenders. Albert DeSalvo – better known as the Boston Strangler – would capture cats and dogs as a child and trap them in boxes, shooting arrows at the defenseless animals for sport.

- **A troubled family history.** Many serial killers come from families with criminal or psychiatric histories or alcoholism. Edmund Kemper killed his grandparents to see what it would be like, and later – after he murdered a string of college students – he killed his alcoholic mother, grinding her vocal chords in the garbage disposal in an attempt to erase the sound of her voice.

- **Childhood abuse.** William Bonin – who killed at least 21 boys and young men in violent rapes and murders – was abandoned as a child, sent to live in a group home where he himself was sexually assaulted. The connections suggest either a rage that can't be erased – Aileen Wuornos, a rare female serial killer, was physically and sexually abused throughout her childhood, resulting in distrust of others and a pent-up rage that exploded during a later rape - or a disassociation of sorts, refusing to connect on a human level with others for fear of being rejected yet again.

- **Substance abuse.** Many serial killers use drugs or alcohol. Jeffrey Dahmer was discharged from the Army due to a drinking problem he developed in high school, and he used alcohol to lure his victims to his apartment, where he killed them in a fruitless effort to create a zombie-like sex slave who would never leave him.

- **Voyeurism.** When Ted Bundy was a teen, he spent his nights as a Peeping Tom, hoping to get a glimpse of one of the neighborhood girls getting undressed in their bedrooms.

- **Serial killers are usually smart.** While their IQ is not usually the reason why serial killers elude police for so long, many have very high IQs. Edmund Kemper was thisclose to being considered a genius (his IQ was 136, just four points beneath the 140 mark that earns genius status), and he used his intelligence to create complex cons that got him released from prison early after killing his grandparents, allowing eight more women to die.
- **Can't keep a job.** Serial killers often have trouble staying employed, either because their off-hours activities take up a lot of time (Jeffrey Dahmer hid bodies in his shower, the shower he used every morning before work, because he was killing at such a fast rate) or because their obsessions have them hunting for victims when they should be on the clock.

Trademarks of a serial killer

While what we know helps us get a better understanding of potential serial killers – and perhaps take a closer look at our weird little neighbors – it is still tricky for police and FBI agents to track serial killers down without knowing a few tells.

The signature

While serial killers like to stake a claim over their killings – "Serial killers typically have some sort of a signature," according to Dr. Scott Bonn, a professor at Drew University in New Jersey – they are usually still quite neat, and a signature does not necessarily mean evidence.

"Jack the Ripper, of course, his signature was the ripping of the bodies," said Bonn.

While there are multiple theories, Jack the Ripper has yet to be identified, despite the similarities in his murders.

Too, the Happy Face Killer, Keith Hunter Jespersen – whose childhood was marked by alcoholic parents, teasing at school and a propensity to abuse small animals - drew happy faces on the numerous letters he sent to both media and authorities, teasing them a bit with a carrot on a string.

"If the forensic evidence itself - depending upon the bones or flesh or whatever is left - if it allows for that sort of identification, that would be one way of using forensic evidence to link these murders," Bonn said.

The cooling off period

Organized killers are so neat, tidy and meticulous that they may never leave clues, even if they have a signature.

And if there's a long cooling off period between crimes, tracking the killer becomes even more of a challenge.

After a murder – which could be compared to a sexual experience or getting high on drugs – the uncontrollable urges that led the killer to act dissipate, at least temporarily.

But according to Ressler, serial killers are rarely satisfied with their kills, and each one increases desire – in the same way a porn addiction can start with the pages of Playboy then turn into BDSM videos or other fetishes when Playboy pictorials are no longer satisfying.

"I was literally singing to myself on my way home, after the killing. The tension, the desire to kill a woman had built up in such explosive proportions that when I finally pulled the trigger, all the pressures, all the tensions, all the hatred, had just vanished, dissipated, but only for a short time," said David Berkowitz, better known as the Son of Sam.

Afterwards, the memory of the murder, or mementos from the murder such as the skulls Jeffrey Dahmer retained, the scalps collected by David Gore or the box of vulvas Ed Gein kept in his kitchen, no longer become enough, and the killers must kill again, creating a "serial" cycle.

That window between crimes usually becomes smaller, however, which allows authorities to notice similarities in murder scenes or methodology, making tracking easier.

In the case of William Bonin, there were months between his first few murders, but toward the end, he sometimes killed two young men a day to satisfy his increasingly uncontrollable urges.

"Sometimes... I'd get tense and think I was gonna go crazy if I couldn't get some release, like my head would explode. So I'd go out hunting. Killing helped me... It was like ... needing to go gambling or getting drunk. I had to do it," Bonin said.

Hunting in pairs

Some serial killers – between 10 and 25 percent - find working as a team more efficient, and they use their charm as the hook to lure in accomplices.

Ed Gein may never have killed anyone had his accomplice, a mentally challenged man who helped Gein dig up the graves of women who resembled his mother, not been sent to a nursing home, leaving Gein unable to dig up the dead on his own.

Texas killer Dean Corll used beer, drugs, money and candy to bribe neighborhood boys to bring him their friends for what they were promised was a party, but instead would turn to torture and murder. He would have killed many more if one of his accomplices had not finally shot him to prevent another night of death.

William Bonin also liked to work with friends, and he enticed boys who were reportedly on the low end of the IQ scale to help him sadistically rape and torture his victims.

Other red flags

According to the FBI's Behavioral Science Unit – founded by Robert Ressler - 60 percent of murderers whose crimes involved sex were childhood bed wetters, and sometimes carried the habit into adulthood. One such serial killer, Alton Coleman, regularly wet his pants, earning the humiliating nickname "Pissy."

Sexual arousal over violent fantasies during puberty can also play a role in a serial killer's future.

Jeffrey Dahmer hit puberty about the same time he was dissecting road kill, so in some way, his wires became crossed and twisted, and sex and death aroused him.

Brain damage? Maybe

While Helen Morrison's test found that John Wayne Gacy's brain was normal, and Jeffrey Dahmer's father never had the opportunity to have his son's brain studied, although both he and Jeffrey had wanted the study, there is some evidence that some serial killers have brain damage that impact their ability to exact rational control.

"Normal parents? Normal brains? I think not," said Dr. Jonathan Pincus, a neurologist and author of the book "Base Instincts: What Makes Killers Kill."

"Abusive experiences, mental illnesses and neurological deficits interplayed to produce the tragedies reported in the newspapers. The most vicious criminals have also been, overwhelmingly, people who have been grotesquely abused as children and have paranoid patterns of thinking," said Pincus in his book, adding that childhood traumas can impact the developmental anatomy and functioning of the brain.

***

So what do we know?

Serial killers can be either uber-smart or brain damaged, completely people savvy or totally awkward, high functioning and seemingly normal or unable to hold down a job.

But essentially, no matter what their back story, their modus operandi or their style, "they're evil," said criminal profiler Pat Brown.

And do we need to know anything more than that?

A Note From The Author

Hello, this is Jack Rosewood. Thank you for reading this true crime story. I hope you enjoyed the read of this chilling story. If you did, I'd appreciate if you would take a few moments to post a review on Amazon.

I would also love if you'd sign up to my newsletter to receive updates on new releases, promotions and a FREE copy of my Herbert Mullin E-Book, www.JackRosewood.com

Thanks again for reading this book, make sure to follow me on Facebook.

A big thanks to Rebecca Lo who helped me write this book.

Best Regards

Jack Rosewood

CPSIA information can be obtained
at www.ICGtesting.com
Printed in the USA
LVHW010104110921
697564LV00012B/613